Squirrel the Stone

a handbook for the creative mind

Pixelated, Written, and Ruined

by

Ami Braverman

About the Author:

I am a reckless raconteur,
riddled with rumination,
a creature confined to the contours,
clammy and crumbling, of my mind.
There is no escape.

Yet in a musty corner
of this airless dungeon,
adjacent to the portrait
of a panda named Carl,
The Porthole of Creation,
where freedom exhales,
rising from the fertilized soil.

And on this wax of bees,
I, on a cedar stool,
My Cathedra,
am at times permitted
to invite others within.
Yes, permitted.

For never have I been asked
if my nature should be thus,
a being so utterly infested,
irresponsible introspections,
a danger to others and self.

And though my creations
do glorify foolery and play,
these stories will, for all posterity
be painted by mine temperament,
that innate cavern –
Addictive Melancholy.

Thus, at the doorway to polite society,
I, a creative satellite, observe,
pondering, squealing commentary,
scribbling notes.

All of the thoughts depicted in this book are real.

While attending Yael's recital,
I started thinking...

...about Squirrel the Stone.

The eclectic Tribeca apartment was an
exposition of radiant appliances, molded
ceilings, fancy cheeses, and industrial pipes,
all displayed amongst a scattering of
portraits in the shadow of Jung.

Grasping a glass,
              authentic red,
                          I deepened my slouch.

I first met Squirrel the Stone at
The Genesis Festival in Megiddo Forest.

Perched in front of the baby grand,
        Yael began expanding on strings,
                how notes can combine.
Was our performer against the idea of
                music being harmonious?

To me, it all sounded like complex chemical
computations, and, as is my nature, I
reformed the words into mine own,
'various voices voyage in harmony but
maybe they should not?'

Following the night, I stumbled through the
flaps of a random tent, mind lingering on
drums and women that smelled of lavender
thrift stores.

There crouched a stranger, a random,
cleanshaven sentinel, smoking a breakfast

joint.

As Yael played, thoughts went further
                                  astray,
     informing   and reforming.

Was this complex music beyond me, like
Tweetsbook?

Homophony vs. polyphony, were they a
dichotomy or two poles on a spectrum?

And why was our hosts' Alsatian staring
                                    at me?

          Am I on the spectrum?

I do often become 'the scientist' as a way
of confronting life's complexities.

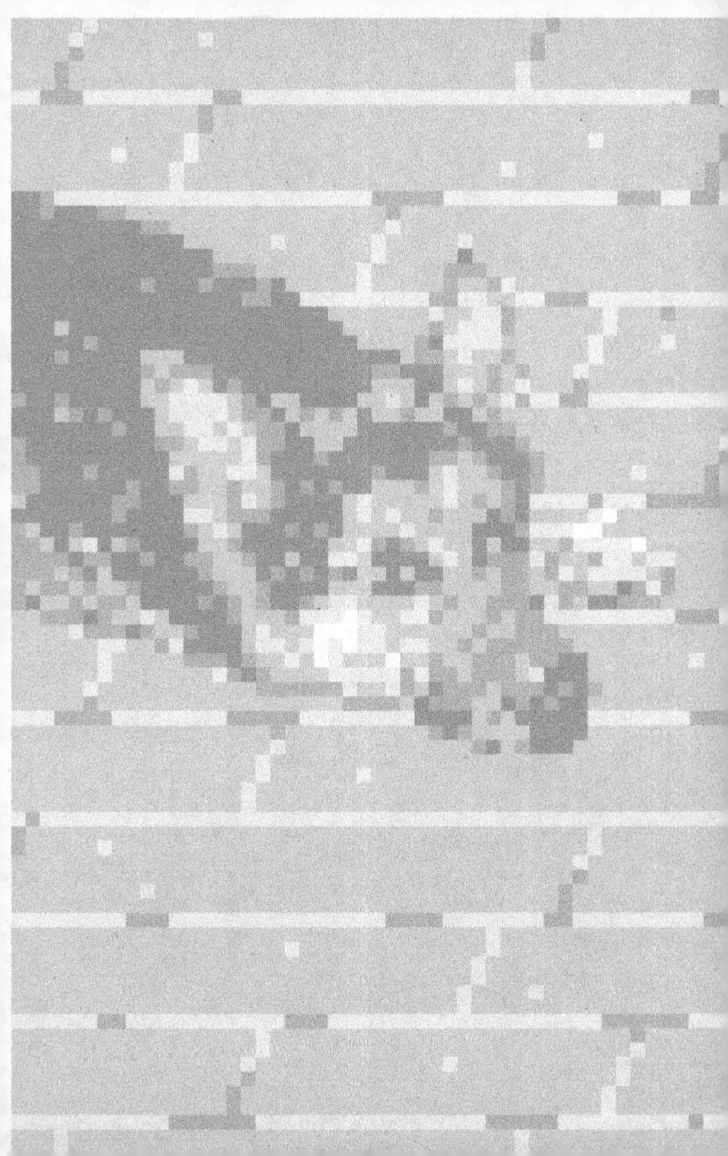

Unraveling,

I found myself

In the middle,

Staring at a stone.

Its name was Squirrel.

To my ears, the piano music sounded
incomplete, almost as though the different
pieces were still being composed.

Elicited was the vivid image of
                              wine on sand.

Beautiful people, vibrant with an excitement of their own existence, flickered by; and, but for Squirrel, I would have joined them.

From time to time, my friends would seek signs of life by giving my motionless body a loving kick.

But again, Squirrel.

I turned to Esther to see if she had
noticed the dog, now licking my shoe.
For some inexplicable reason, my wife was
directing towards me a loving, possibly proud
expression, touching but also just a little
bit creepy.
How long had she been staring like that?

No matter. At least she had not noticed
my earlier incident with our hosts,
Yet another awkward scene that will need
to travel with me to the grave.

This grim suitcase of faux pas is getting
pretty pretty full.

But why had I been that nervous?
So, they were both analysts. And? So what?
I am a psychologist myself.
Should not I be immune to that primitive
fear of psychodynamic 'x-ray vision'?

Or is it true that the cobbler goes
                              barefoot?

My feet were aching from the night before.
Back then, I was into that whole
'real hippies dance barefoot' scene.

As I pondered Squirrel, it became evident
that there was always more to see.

Details formed in my mind.

Squirrel had a plateau, all across the left side, smooth...

...and in total contrast to the crumbling ridges t'wards the peak.

A curly haired and perky belly-dancer twirled by, casting a silk rag over my laying corpse. Later, for many years, I would use it as a purple belt.

Real hippies dance barefoot.

Center stage, towards the base, I examined a thin band, fused into the rich, earthy gray that was Squirrel. Was this an ancient marriage of material, an integral part of the whole, or was it a parasite, destroying Squirrel from within?

This blackened fault-line worried me.

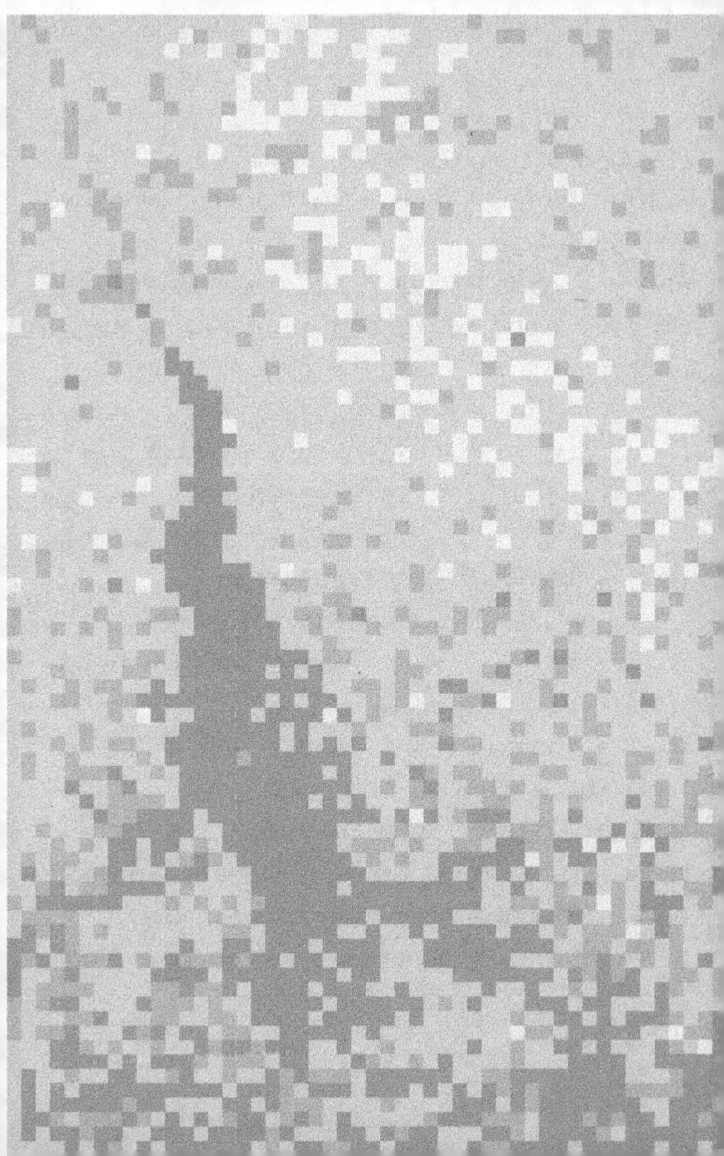

Escaped a curl, untamed, unfurled, as the
woman davened over that mahogany machine
- creating.
And the room gradually became condensed
with her pianistic echoes, as hands argued,
each trying to steal the plot.

I was suddenly reminded of a train of
thought that invariably returns.

Do the footpaths of creativity
          always wind through that same
                              bottomless ravine?

Having thoroughly immersed myself in life,
from successfully selling socks in a
gas station to exchanging with artists,
physicists, writers, fighters, daters, waiters,
and many many more, and Rabbis, I always
seem to catch glimpses of that same Abyss.

                                        m

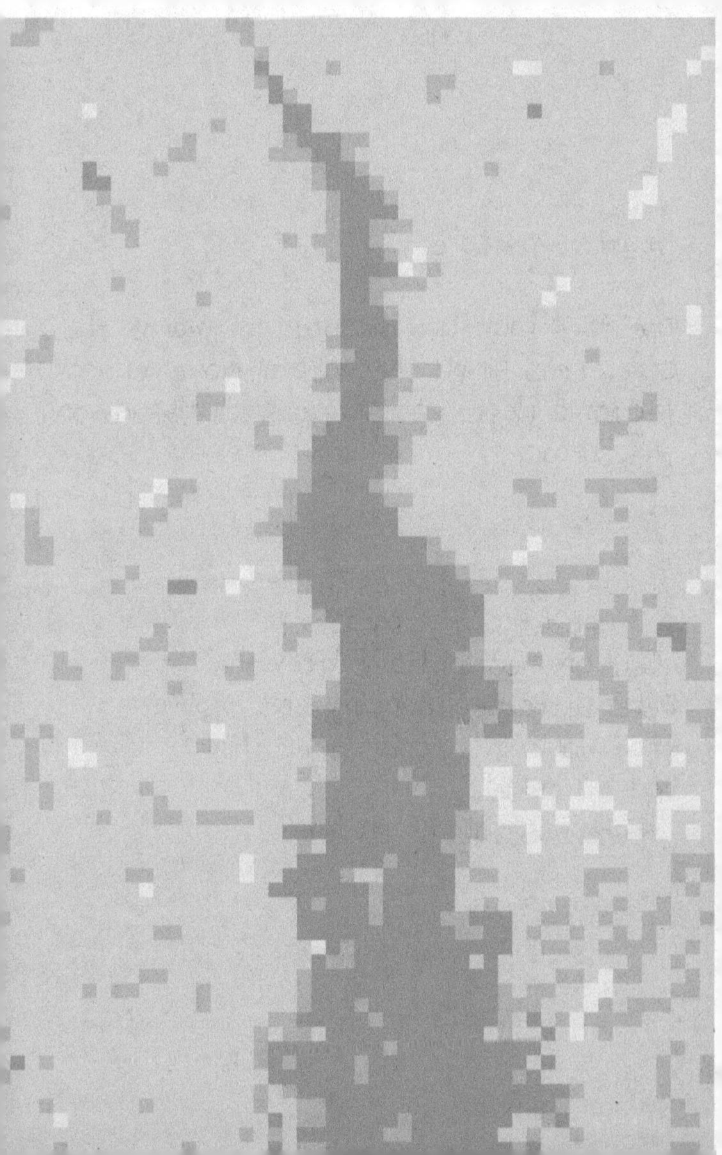

Squirrel was safe.

The dark fault-line did not go t'wards the core. 'Twas simply the natural movement of tectonic plates, causing a small fissure on the surface.

Maybe I was the parasite?
Out on medical leave from the Defense Force, dancing and doping?
What would my grandmother think?
But my ankle...
there was talk of surgery.

In the night to come, the second intifada would break out. That is not a part of this story, although maybe it is? Because, as I kept on exploring Squirrel's slopes, hour after hour, I gradually became awash with a sense of dread.

With sweat upon my pits, I now pondered, maybe I had caused the second intifada? Was the metaphysical education, relayed upon me by my mother, a thing?

More importantly, could our psychoanalyst hosts catch glimpses of my sourceless contrition?

Guilt, as is its nature, consumed.

But was it truly without a source?

Could I have saved him?

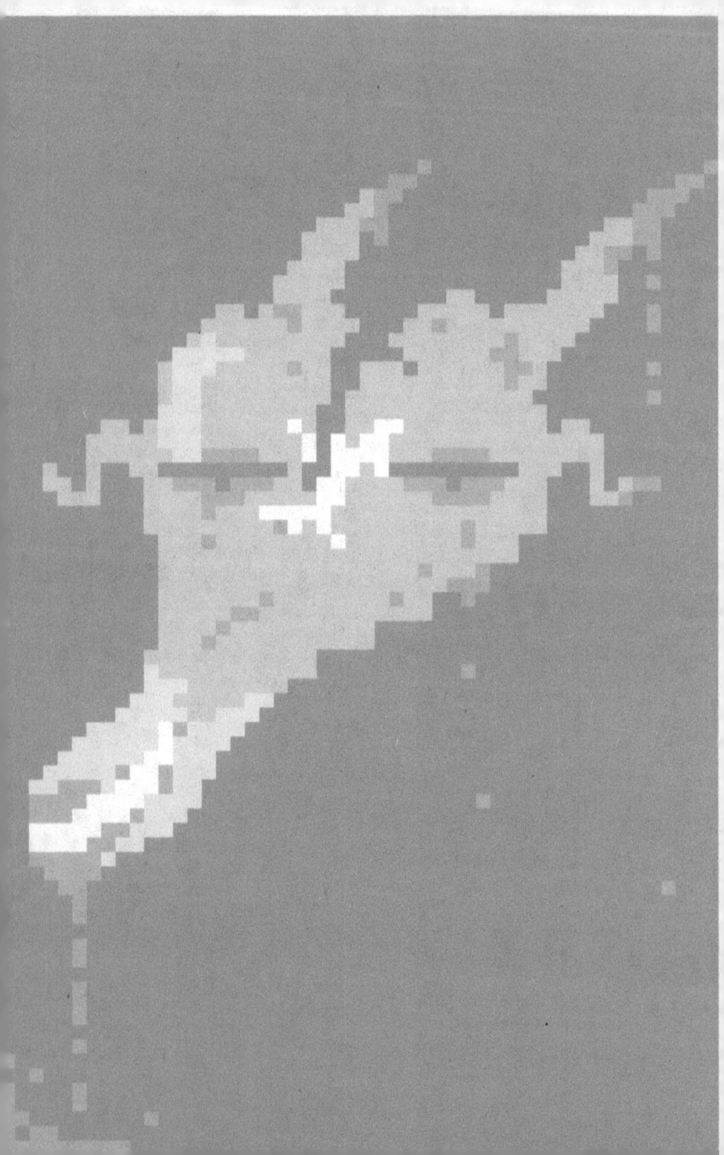

Generatia.
Oh.
This abiding enmity,
internecine echo,
muddy lungs,
teeth in tract,
canst thou truly be mine own?

Canst thou?

Esther lay her hand

upon my shoulder.

My grandmother once confided in us that,
every night, Saba and she would lay in bed,
making each other laugh.

Esther and I have a wordless understanding
that ours is a very similar connection,
perhaps because we both were clearly
to that time, meant to be.

a tint of play within our gray
With just a thirteen-year delay,
at once, you were my night, my day.
Thus twine our souls 'pon kitchen walls,
and t'wards where 'twas pictured halls.
A voiceless sound and we were found.
The path of us rewards the ground.

The other night, we left an online review for
a badly made tile cutter:

'It gave us diarrhea.'

That bottomless ravine, The Abyss where the act of Creation lies, is a mystical realm where reality meets the vast unknown, and I do not think that the two are in harmony.

As a child, began I to write poems, and upon discovering that indefinable space, foolishly, did not look away. Barely did I survive. Instead, began I to pull on the threads of dangerous thoughts -

'Why can I only fall asleep when not trying to?'

'If you focus too long on your breathing, can you stop?'

'Memory needs time, but does time need memory?'

'Does evil exist...   in me?'

A childhood friend of mine died from a similar irresponsible introspection.

I sometimes wonder if he had been one of those masters who can replace the mechanics of technique with the nuances of plain artistry and lingering style, overwhelming in their humanity and, too often, prone to reckless treks through that same bottomless ravine.

A torrent of recursive signals is life.
And us, ordinary beings, we communicate our
intellects through the patterns we arrange
out of this multi-sensory deluge.

The intelligent amongst us form arcane
impressions, only partially visible to the less
endowed, who, hidden from harm, wonder at
these seemingly unpredictable tapestries.
But there are limits to intelligence. For no
matter how elusive the design, a pattern
does exist, 'neath a liftable veil. Therefore,
the concept of intelligence is inevitably
doomed to the predictable and the benign.

And then, there are the few, those genius
farmhands, toiling in the fields of creation,
planting seeds of random, smoothing earth.

The result of their compositions?
From which to forge patterns of our own,
a torrent of recursive signals.

When entering university, I noticed how even seemingly solid facts can still fall within the realm of the uncertain.

It was almost as though The Abyss of Creation may, itself, question reality, unraveling whoever may stumble upon it.

Or is it 'whomever'?

Ohad.

Further down the road of my academic career, in the warmth of Nachshon's lab of Brain and Cognition, I began to study that place again, but with more caution, using a buffer of logic, rational, and intellect.

However, measure the space, I could not, for it would not be defined.

I, creator, do not write what I know.
Rather, what I did not know was there.

Sense I, loitering, hiding within,
the thoughts before the words.

All of them, in my skull,
depth unknown, an absorbing lake.

Booklet blue, hidden in this pocket,
etched with pen, my mind.

In my short life, I have waited
to move back in.

Then, as an adult writer reborn, surrounded
by a cloudless, sunny day, and with every
single light turned on, I named it, and
renamed it, and renamed it, and renamed it,
and renamed it...

and renamed it...

and renamed it...

Rhetorus.
Give us neither direction,
nor a purpose, nor light.
Give not sight.
Illume not the road.
Take your notes, if you must,
by dark night.

Peppermint eclipse tattoos
are nostalgic of what?
Rhetorus.
Trampling yellow bricks,
we decipher the haze -
that is us.

We follow the trail of words,
a network of vapor,
by our pulse,
read fog, which you can't,
the beat of our sand,
nowhere else.

Nature. Art. Metaphor. Symbols. Aleph-bet.
The Drawing Board. Thoughts outside of the
box. The Force behind forced connections.
Brainstorms. Swimming in the vast unknown.
The infinite Void. The edge of reality. Space
between particles. The Abyss of Creation.
That bottomless ravine. Setting.
                        The places we disappear †
The Lateral Dimension. Golden fields where
one can gather wool. Grey areas, or should
that be areas of gray? I can't decide.
Questioning Faith. Free Will. Decorating fate.
Alternate endings. Fuzzy logic. F = T ∇ St.
Summarizing Chaos. Fuzzy magic. True Rando .
Dawson's Philosophy. Being captivated by
a tale. Being. Play. The sound between one
thought and another. A sequence of notes
humming in all our heads. Blank stares
out of a moving vehicle. Silent walks in
the desert, experiencing umami of the mind.
Collected memories of a human past.
The exact moment, when a mother is born,
and a child is given.

Pixels on a canvas.

shapes in the **shadows.**

their clouds.

that children give

The names

Play.
Stories.
Ever after.
Never before.
In the beginning,
there was the beginning.
And thus, both the concepts of Logic
and Time were introduced, as, too,
was the notion of concepts.

Of course, notions require a mind to
inhabit. Whereupon, together with a mind,
Space appeared, taking up quite a lot of
itself, prompting Time to politely state that
it had been there first.
To which Space responded, "duh."

Time, taking umbrage at the tone, began to
pout, loudly. Sound whirred into existence.
Then Space, never one to let things pass,
pointed out that Time had just insinuated
that it had in fact inhabited a 'there'.

In response, Time, the eternal bully, ganged up with Sound and began yelling, making sure to mention Space's large, um, physique.

The mind, just created and already home to thoughts that clearly could not get along, asked for some clarity. Then there was light.

Logic, feeling weighed down by accumulated dust (likely due to lack of use) and, frankly, quite sick of all the commotion, ran out 'just' for a pack of cigarettes, conveniently leaving its wallet at home, something that would become a lifelong habit. Hello Motion.

As you most likely know, Light immediately became totally infatuated with Motion, who was, of course, secretly in love with Space's plump mass. This original love triangle would be the cause of much confusion for all physicists of the future, even, no, especially the very very smart ones (at one point in time, referred to as nerds).

Incidentally, have any of you heard that a triangle is the strongest shape in the world? Coincidence? I think not.

Mathematics, Logic's younger brother, reared his ugly little head, making sure to be condescending towards Belief, at every possible opportunity.

Gender sauntered in, to the dismay of, well, everybody.

The mind, a bit slower than its own thoughts and already a recovering alcoholic, finally asked a scary question, with disastrous consequences, followed by a much much scarier one.

"Am I alone?"

"Am I a nerd?"

To which Frank responded, "Yes."

Surface Adult

Yet I recall a time when time was slower,
dreams were tangible,
and poems would rhyme.

Living a narrative without a plot,
or a plot without a narrative,
I sibilate to a blackened screen.
Whereupon have I become this surface adult,
yearning vague for childlike engagement?
And why are there so many more like me?

For we recall a time when time was slower,
dreams were tangible,
and poems would rhyme.

Storybooks were real, once upon a time.

The essence of a story lies much less within the movements of the plot, as it does in the distractions thereof.

In the telling of a narrative, the hero's actions are the forward momentum towards an inevitable, final release. Yet, in ways, these are the most benign elements of storytelling, for they are shackled and chained, fettered to the needs of the journey.

Random, scattered scenes of distraction are arguably more material and enriching than any climax brought on by actions bound to plot, for they uncover a pureness of intent on the author's part.
Imagine an unseen neighbor's rant about her uncle's addiction to apples, the bumper sticker on a squatter's exercise bike, a kid-sized banjo thrown atop the coffin of a six-year-old girl, or simply the floral dress of juror number five.

Yes, the true personality of a story lies
within the distractions, for in these
instances, nothing governs a character's
enterprises other than their own inner
urges. No journey is required,
only expression of self.

Wait.

What was I thinking, again?

Oh, right. When was the last time I ate?

Stomach screaming to what may have been the beat, I was getting increasingly fearful about the cheese.

Is it customary to get fancy food also at the end of a recital? Or do you only get snacks in the beginning?

After University, while becoming a therapist,
I sensed this place again and utilized it as
a tool to help others face their own
internal conflicts. I learned to stuff a piece
of that space into a box of sand, where a
person may explore the thoughts in their
mind - relatively safe from harm.

Guilt, as is its nature, consumes.

Could I have helped him?

Yael's music still sounded unfinished to me and yet, without a doubt, it was music. The compositions were meandering through that ravine, both real and unreal, as they questioned their own existence.

That was what I was thinking about as I listened to Yael's recital. I was there, once again, studying all the faces of Squirrel the Stone, every nook and every cranny, every cleft and every monocline, even those two intriguing alluvial fans 'pon the right.

Only this time,

I was the stone.

Acknowledgements:

Ella Bar-El, my mother,
You always let my thoughts be free.
And thus, you created me.

Nachshon Meiran, my mentor,
I do believe that your lab saved my mind.
I am so very thankful.

Ohad Remer, my friend, I miss you.
It hurts.

Notes:

I linger on the dreamy flow,
that precedes a thought,
like waves upon a silver string,

tenuous but taut.

Notes:

I linger on the dreamy flow,
that precedes a thought,
like waves upon a silver string,

tenuous but taut.

Notes:

I linger on the dreamy flow,
that precedes a thought,
like waves upon a silver string,

tenuous but taut.

Notes:

Notes:

Notes:

Notes:

Dedication:

Esther, my friend, my wife,
mother of our people, mentor,

You seeing me, is that truly about me?
Is bread about the baker?
And the baker? Is the baker the bread?
Because self is a representation and
representation is the only form of self.
That is human; that is art.

Then again, can you really separate the
creation from the creator, or the creator
from the creation?

I am not intellectualizing.
This is personal, don't you see?
I am trapped in my cave, sitting on a chair
that does not feel like mine own. And the
soil reeks. And Carl is no comfort at all.
But you are. Standing in your own cave,
peeking into mine, as I stare into yours.
If anyone is a comfort, it is you.

That is the human paradox, is it not?
The personal can only truly exist through
the porthole of human connection. Do you
and I appear as a consequence of mutual
creation? A synergy of personalities, like
brass trumpets to puffy cheeks?

By the way, I see you yawning there. But
that is the point. I know that you know all
of this. And, you know that I know that you
know that I know that you know this.
You know?

Fine. I will have to show the banana.
Because no science or philosophy can really
explain why yellow potassium inside a rubbery,
crescent shaped skin is innately funny.
No, a sincere story needs to be shown,
not explained.

You and I connect, we fit, like a mirror
inside a fridge. Why? Because both of us
could think of truly valid reasons why the
inside of a fridge would need a mirror.
Maybe the cheese likes to look its best in
the morning? Maybe guilty pleasures should
only be gotten with the toll of seeing
the shame inside our own eyes?

We fit. Because addressing a postcard to
you, as you sit in the back seat of our
friend's car is funny to us both, intuitively.

We fit. Because screaming through our
snorkels, "how is this fun?" has become a
statement embroidered on our souls and
physically in our two sons' bedroom.

Crooked teeth at our wedding and romantic
portraits next to NYC trash cans, so iconic.
A crowbar pen to sign the ketubah.

Immigrating with one border collie, 19 socks, and 263 books, heavy heavy books. Our first car, purchased from an intensely agitated farmer. We couldn't allow ourselves cherry tomatoes yet, but we absolutely had to install a tropical headliner in that jeep.

Jigsaw puzzles when mourning, and Yom Kippur too. Cowboy boots, only for display. Smiling at the elderly. A wooden writer's block for my 40th. An evil rock that is clearly a muse and/or Saba's ear. Three weeks, 12 returns, and 97 miles to find the perfect computer mouse.
Double that for a travel pillow.
Quadruple for the right first year gifts.

Serenity now.

Philosoph Dawson.

Taking our summers in a concentration camp. But of course. And your script with no words. Because how could you possibly find an adequate voice for all that might have been gained, but was taken away? Now, fearing for the future of our children.

Feeling comfortable, addictive melancholy, yours and mine. Because no-one has ever asked us if our natures should be thus, beings so infested with irresponsible introspections. Yet you and I, we fit.

Like funny is to a banana, Esther, we fit. Because I see you in your cave and you see me, in mine. We are home in each other. And look how beautiful our synergy has become.

It is simply impossible to voice everything - that has been gained.

www.ingramcontent.com/pod-product-compliance
Lightning Source LLC
Chambersburg PA
CBHW012027110726
47995CB00006B/1163